BiG Thoughts for Little Thinkers

BiG Thoughts for Little Thinkers

BiG Thoughts for Little Thinkers

BiG Thoughts for Little Thinkers

BiG Thoughts for Little Thinkers

BiG Thoughts for Little Thinkers

BiG Thoughts for Little Thinkers

BiG Thoughts for Little Thinkers

BiG Thoughts for Little Thinkers

To our darling
Andrea,

BiG Thoughts for Little Thinkers

With all our love, ♡
Aunt Tricia, Uncle David, Bethany,
Mandie, Kenny + Timmy

THE GOSPEL
BY JOEY ALLEN

New Leaf Press

First Printing: March 2005
Second Printing: March 2007

For more information write:
New Leaf Press Inc., PO Box 726, Green Forest, AR 72638
Illustrations and text by Joey Allen

For my mom

ISBN-13: 978-0-89221-617-8
ISBN-10: 0-89221-617-4
Library of Congress Control Number: 2004118202
Printed in Italy

FOREWORD

Knowing how to tell a child about believing in Jesus Christ is a precious opportunity that starts with a loving touch. How beautiful was the approach of Jesus when He responded so graciously to the people who brought their infants, eager to have Him touch them (Luke 18:15-16). Before our children ever understand our words, we will have clearly communicated through a loving touch.

Joining loving words with a loving touch, however, is a challenge. You don't want to tell them so much that they are confused. What are the essentials? Who was Jesus Christ? What do I need to believe about Him to become a Christian? Why do I need to become a Christian? These questions exercised our minds and hearts regularly. Joey's *Big Thoughts for Little Thinkers* gives help.

We have four children. There are two pairs of them, two years apart and four and one half years between the pairs. Having devotions with them was a challenge. We finally hit upon the habit of having two devotional times. The older kids could sit in on the devotions with the younger kids, and the younger kids could sit in with the older kids. Most nights, everyone was present during each devotion time. That way the younger kids heard more advanced ideas and the responses of the older children. That may be why the younger children came to the Lord at an earlier age than the older ones.

This book by Joey Allen is an excellent tool with carefully chosen words and eye-catching art. It will be of significant value in helping you make the Gospel simple enough so that younger children can understand the gift of salvation, but also advanced enough for older children to delve into the rich truths of God's Word for themselves. We wish we had had books like this when our children were small, but now we look forward to using *Big Thoughts for Little Thinkers* with our grandchildren.

– Earl and Ruth Radmacher
President Emeritus
Western Seminary

A WORD TO PARENTS AND TEACHERS

Out of the overflow of the love shared between the members of the Trinity, God created us. God created us to love Him. Despite our rebellion against God, and at great expense to himself, God sent His Son so we could once again fulfill the purpose for which He created us. Paul summarized the crux of the gospel message, the good news, in 1 Corinthians 15:3–5, "I delivered to you as of first importance what I also received, that Christ died for our sins according to the Scriptures, and that He was buried, and that He was raised on the third day according to the Scriptures, and that He appeared." Christ's death paid for our sins, and His resurrection ensures that we, too, will experience resurrection. Is that good news, or what!

The Bible affirms the value of grounding children in the gospel from an early age. Paul endorsed the teaching his protégé Timothy received from his mother, Eunice, and his grandmother, Lois. Paul encouraged him, "Continue in the things you have learned and become convinced of, knowing from whom you have learned them, and that *from childhood* you have known the sacred writings which are able to give you the wisdom that leads to salvation through faith which is in Christ Jesus" (2 Timothy 3:14–15, emphasis added).

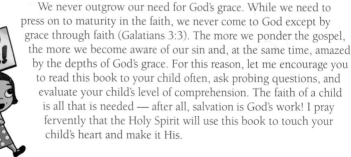

We never outgrow our need for God's grace. While we need to press on to maturity in the faith, we never come to God except by grace through faith (Galatians 3:3). The more we ponder the gospel, the more we become aware of our sin and, at the same time, amazed by the depths of God's grace. For this reason, let me encourage you to read this book to your child often, ask probing questions, and evaluate your child's level of comprehension. The faith of a child is all that is needed — after all, salvation is God's work! I pray fervently that the Holy Spirit will use this book to touch your child's heart and make it His.

– Joey Allen

Hi! My name is Gracie. I want to tell you the best news in the whole world. The best news is that God loves you, and He wants you to be with Him forever.

John 3:16

God created the whole world. He made trees and colors and puppy dogs!

Genesis 1:1-31; Isaiah 45:18; Hebrews 11:3; John 1:3

God created you, too. God knows your name. God knows what makes you happy and what makes you sad. He cares about you very much.

Psalm 139:13; Isaiah 43:1; 1 Peter 5:7

God wants you to be happy by being with Him. Real happiness only comes from God.

Psalm 16:11; Zephaniah 3:17; Philippians 4:4

When you try to be happy without God, you do bad things called "sin." You sin with your words, your thoughts, and your actions. You do bad things because you have a sinful heart.

Isaiah 53:6; Jeremiah 2:12-13; 17:9

Have you ever been punished for disobeying your parents? If you have done just one sin, you have disobeyed God and deserve to be punished.

Ezekiel 18:4; Revelation 21:8

The punishment for sin is separation from God. You cannot go to heaven because you have done bad things. This is a big problem.

Isaiah 59:2; Romans 3:10-18, 23

But I have good news for you! God loves you so much that He made a way for you to be with Him in heaven one day!

John 14:6; Romans 5:8

God sent His Son, Jesus, to the earth to be born as a baby. Jesus became human, but He was still completely God. Jesus grew up just like you and me, but He never did anything mean or bad.

Colossians 1:15; 2:9; Hebrews 1:3; 4:15; 1 John 4:14

Pretend that a car is about to hit you, but then your friend pushes you out of the way. Your friend loves you so much that he saves you from getting hurt by the car, but he gets hurt instead.

Jesus loved you so much that He died in your place. Jesus did not deserve to die, but He died on the cross to take your punishment.

Isaiah 53:6;
2 Corinthians 5:21; 1 Peter 3:18

Three days after Jesus died, He came back to life and lots of people saw Him! Then Jesus went up to heaven.

*Psalm 16:10; Mark 16:6;
1 Corinthians 15:3-7*

Jesus is alive, and He wants to give you eternal life in heaven. Eternal life is a free gift that lasts forever and ever. You can have the free gift of eternal life by trusting in Jesus.

Acts 16:31; Romans 6:23

Many people think they must be good to go to heaven. But no one is good enough to go to heaven.

Ephesians 2:8–9; Titus 3:5; Romans 3:10

Being good does not take away your sins. Jesus is the only One who can take away the sin that separates you from God.

Isaiah 64:6; 2 Timothy 1:9

The only thing you must do is trust in Jesus. When you trust in Jesus, He will give you the free gift of eternal life.

Romans 4:5; 10:13

When you ride in an airplane, you don't need to flap your arms or jump up and down. You cannot help the airplane fly. All you need to do is trust the airplane to get you where you need to go.

In the same way, there is nothing you can do to get to heaven on your own. You cannot save yourself. All you need to do is trust Jesus to take you to heaven.

John 5:24; 20:31

When you trust in Jesus, He will give you a home in heaven. Even if you die, you will come back to life — just like Jesus did!

John 14:1–3; Romans 6:5; 1 Corinthians 15:20–22; 2 Corinthians 5:1

When you trust in Jesus, He forgives your sins. God will erase the bad things you have done so that nothing will separate you from Him.

Psalm 32:1; 103:12; Isaiah 43:25;
Micah 7:19; Colossians 2:14

Before you trust in Jesus, sin bosses you around. After you trust in Jesus, He sets you free from sin so that you can love and obey Him.

Colossians 2:13; Romans 6:1-14

When you trust in Jesus, He makes you a child of God. God will be your Father, and you will always be His child.

Psalm 73:23-24; John 1:12; Romans 8:15-17

Even when you do bad things, God never stops loving you. He has promised to love you no matter what!

John 10:28–29; Romans 8:38–39

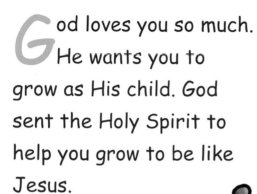

God loves you so much. He wants you to grow as His child. God sent the Holy Spirit to help you grow to be like Jesus.

2 Corinthians 1:21-22; Ephesians 1:13

You will grow as God's child as you spend time with Him. Spend time letting God talk to you through the Bible. You can talk to God anytime and anywhere and He will hear your prayers!

Jeremiah 33:3; 2 Timothy 3:16–17; 1 Peter 2:2

Thank you for letting me tell you the best news in the world. I hope you share this good news with your friends.

Matthew 28:19-20

AFTERWORD FOR PARENTS AND TEACHERS

Long before I could swim, I used to throw myself off the diving board into the deep end of the pool. I jumped with the kind of reckless abandon that could only be explained by the confidence I had in my Dad's waiting arms. I believed that he would catch me, and he always did. This kind of trusting dependence, this kind of faith, is typical of children. In fact, according to a recent study by George Barna, nearly half of all American Christians trusted in Jesus as their Savior by the age of twelve. We should never discount a child's potential for faith.

As you read this book to your child and talk about the Good News, pray for your child and for wisdom. Be sensitive to the working of the Holy Spirit in your child's heart. The decision to trust in Jesus is the most important decision your child will ever make. When your child is ready, provide an opportunity for him to express his trust in Jesus in the form of a prayer. A prayer can be a tangible and memorable expression of trust. Your child may say a personal prayer or you could guide your child with a prayer like this:

> Dear God in heaven, I know I have disobeyed You. I cannot get to heaven on my own. But thank You for loving me and sending Your Son Jesus. I believe that Jesus died on the cross for me. I believe that He came back to life. I trust in Jesus, and only Jesus, to take away my sin, and give me a home in heaven. Amen.

If your child responds to God's grace, rejoice in his decision! Help him grow in faith by reviewing the promises God has made. Help him remember this special occasion. You may want to mark the date in a calendar or Bible. You could even throw a party celebrating your child's spiritual birthday every year. Encourage your child to tell his family and friends. This will cement the decision in your child's mind. Also, if your child makes a decision to trust in Jesus, we would love to rejoice with you! Please contact us at joeyandchristyallen@hotmail.com.

"Jesus called the children to Him and said, "Let the little children come to me, and do not hinder them, for the kingdom of God belongs to such as these" (Luke 18:16).

Also available in this series:

ISBN: 0-89221-614-X

ISBN: 0-89221-615-8

ISBN: 0-89221-616-6

Available at Christian bookstores nationwide